The God Really Loves You Book Series™ Presents:

GOD
Really
Loves You
and
He Gave You the Bible!

**Written and Illustrated
by Wendy Nelson**

God Really Loves You Book Series™ presents:

GOD Really Loves You
and He Gave You the Bible!

Text Copyright ©2022 by Wendy Nelson
Artwork Copyright ©2022 by Wendy Nelson

Published by MediaTek Grafx
POB 62, Bonnieville, Kentucky, 42713

ISBN 978-1-0880-2955-8

Design and production by MediaTek Grafx, Bonnieville, Kentucky
Special thanks to Joan Swan for loving review, critique and advice

The Publisher has made every effort to avoid errors or omissions. Opinions, stories, and themes are intended for entertainment, motivation for research and future study. This book includes content that is non-fiction.

All Scripture quotations are from the The Holy Bible, King James Version, Pradis Software Rel 02.04.03, Built with Conform Version 5.00.0051, Version 5.1.50 Copyright ©2002 The Zondervan Corporation All Rights Reserved.

All rights reserved. This Publication may not be reproduced in whole or in part, stored or transmitted by any means. Media may use small portions for reviews. Please request written permission from Publisher for any other reason.

Printed in the United States of America

A Special Gift for

_____

From

_____

Note

_____
_____
_____

Date

_____

God really loves you!

God is your Father in Heaven.

God is holy and special.

He is three persons in one:
God the Father,
God the Son, Jesus,
and
God the Holy Spirit.

Matthew 28:19-20 Go ye therefore, and teach all nations, baptizing them in the name of the Father, and of the Son, and of the Holy Ghost: 20 Teaching them to observe all things whatsoever I have commanded you: and, lo, I am with you alway, even unto the end of the world. Amen.

God spoke to men and they wrote God's words down.

The Word of God is called the Bible and it was created to help us.

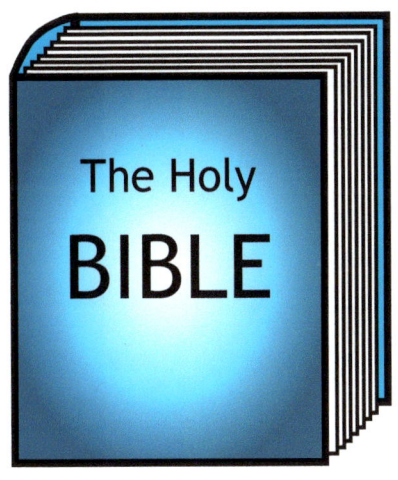

The Bible is about God's love for us!

Isaiah 30:8 Now go, write it before them in a table, and note it in a book, that it may be for the time to come for ever and ever:

Jeremiah 30:2 Thus speaketh the LORD God of Israel, saying, Write thee all the words that I have spoken unto thee in a book.

The holy Bible
has two parts:
it has the Old Testament
and the New Testament.

The
Old Testament
has 39 books.

The
New Testament
has 27 books.

That is a total
of 66 books
in the Bible.

Luke 24:27 And beginning at Moses and all the prophets, he expounded unto them in all the scriptures the things concerning himself.

John 5:39 Search the scriptures; for in them ye think ye have eternal life: and they are they which testify of me.

The Bible is the inspired Word of God. God spoke to man through the Holy Spirit.

God spoke to men called prophets in the Old Testament.

God and Jesus spoke to men called apostles in the New Testament.

2 Peter 1:20-21 Knowing this first, that no prophecy of the scripture is of any private interpretation. 21 For the prophecy came not in old time by the will of man: but holy men of God spake as they were moved by the Holy Ghost.

Prophets wrote down God's words. The words revealed God's love, God's warnings, and God's plans!

The prophets told us about God's Son, Jesus, long before He was born.

John 5:46-47 For had ye believed Moses, ye would have believed me: for he wrote of me. 47 But if ye believe not his writings, how shall ye believe my words?

Deuteronomy 18:18 I will raise them up a Prophet from among their brethren, like unto thee, and will put my words in his mouth; and he shall speak unto them all that I shall command him.

Apostles were appointed by God to study with Jesus.

God's Son, Jesus, taught the 12 apostles. The apostles loved Jesus and followed Him.

The apostles wrote the gospels and letters to people at churches. Their letters speak about correction, love, and hope. They told everyone what Jesus taught them.

Romans 1:1 Paul, a servant of Jesus Christ, called to be an apostle, separated unto the gospel of God,

2 Timothy 3:16-17 All scripture is given by inspiration of God, and is profitable for doctrine, for reproof, for correction, for instruction in righteousness:
17 That the man of God may be perfect, thoroughly furnished unto all good works.

God gives us rules in the Bible.
He tells us what to do and what not to do.

God gave us the Holy Spirit to comfort us, and to help us!

John 14:15-16 If ye love me, keep my commandments. 16 And I will pray the Father, and he shall give you another Comforter, that he may abide with you for ever;

Matthew 4:4 But he answered and said, It is written, Man shall not live by bread alone, but by every word that proceedeth out of the mouth of God.

God loves us so much! He wants us to love Him with all of our heart!

God wants us to listen to Him, and to read the Bible.

God wants us to pray to Him.

God wants us to be thankful for everything He provides.

God wants us to praise Him because He is holy.

God wants us to sing to Him when we are happy.

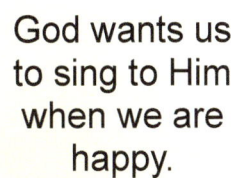

Ephesians 6:7-8 With good will doing service, as to the Lord, and not to men: 8 Knowing that whatsoever good thing any man doeth, the same shall he receive of the Lord, whether he be bond or free.

Zephaniah 3:17 The LORD thy God in the midst of thee is mighty; he will save, he will rejoice over thee with joy; he will rest in his love, he will joy over thee with singing.

We should read the Bible.
God tells us how to live in a good way,
and to love each other.

We are all children of God!
God has done wonderful things for us.

1 John 3:11 For this is the message that ye heard from the beginning, that we should love one another.

Isaiah 12:5 Sing unto the LORD; for he hath done excellent things: this is known in all the earth.

We can choose to love God.
We can choose to love Jesus in our heart!

The Bible tells us that God sent His only Son, Jesus, to help us!

As we get older, if we love and accept Jesus, we will go to a beautiful place called heaven!

John 3:16 For God so loved the world, that he gave his only begotten Son, that whosoever believeth in him should not perish, but have everlasting life.

John 14:1-2 Let not your heart be troubled: ye believe in God, believe also in me. 2 In my Father's house are many mansions: if it were not so, I would have told you. I go to prepare a place for you.

When we are sorry we do something bad, we can change our behavior.

We can tell our Father in Heaven about it!

The Bible says God will forgive us!

Acts 3:19 Repent ye therefore, and be converted, that your sins may be blotted out,

1 Corinthians 10:13 There hath no temptation taken you but such as is common to man: but God is faithful, who will not suffer you to be tempted above that ye are able; but will with the temptation also make a way to escape, that ye may be able to bear it.

The Bible tells us that God loves children, and that each child has an angel!

An angel can protect you.

If we feel weak or scared, God will be strong for us. He is always with us!

That means we are never alone!

Matthew 18:10 Take heed that ye despise not one of these little ones; for I say unto you, That in heaven their angels do always behold the face of my Father which is in heaven.

Joshua 1:9 Have not I commanded thee? Be strong and of a good courage; be not afraid, neither be thou dismayed: for the LORD thy God is with thee whithersoever thou goest.

In the Bible, there are so many exciting stories! God uses stories to teach us many things.

Daniel and the Lion's Den
God protected Daniel from lions!

Noah's Ark
Noah trusted God and built the ark!

Daniel 6:22 My God hath sent his angel, and hath shut the lions' mouths, that they have not hurt me: forasmuch as before him innocency was found in me;

Hebrews 11:7 By faith Noah, being warned of God of things not seen as yet, moved with fear, prepared an ark to the saving of his house; by the which he condemned the world, and became heir of the righteousness which is by faith.

Hebrews 11:30 By faith the walls of Jericho fell down, after they were compassed about seven days.

Matthew 14:19-20 And he commanded the multitude to sit down on the grass, and took the five loaves, and the two fishes, and looking up to heaven, he blessed, and brake, and gave the loaves to his disciples, and the disciples to the multitude. 20 And they did all eat, and were filled:

Mark 4:39-40 And he arose, and rebuked the wind, and said unto the sea, Peace, be still. And the wind ceased, and there was a great calm. 40 And he said unto them, Why are ye so fearful? how is it that ye have no faith?

Not everyone believes God wrote the Bible to save people.

God loves everyone! He is patiently waiting for people to choose to love Him.

2 Peter 3:9 The Lord is not slack concerning his promise, as some men count slackness; but is longsuffering to us-ward, not willing that any should perish, but that all should come to repentance.

The Bible says
that our Father in Heaven wants us
to love Him as a child.
We are all children of God!

We can all grow up in God's love!
We can learn about God, Jesus, and the Holy Spirit!

Ask someone to read the Bible to you!

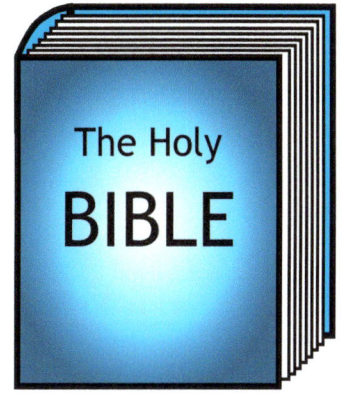

The Holy BIBLE

Matthew 18:3 And said, Verily I say unto you, Except ye be converted, and become as little children, ye shall not enter into the kingdom of heaven.

2 Peter 3:18 But grow in grace, and in the knowledge of our Lord and Saviour Jesus Christ. To him be glory both now and for ever. Amen.

God Really Loves You Book Series™

GodReallyLovesYou.com

Matthew 3:16-17 Jesus, when he was baptized, went up straightway out of the water: and, lo, the heavens were opened unto him, and he saw the Spirit of God descending like a dove, and lighting upon him: 17 And lo a voice from heaven, saying, This is my beloved Son, in whom I am well pleased.

Matthew 18:3-5 And said, Verily I say unto you, Except ye be converted, and become as little children, ye shall not enter into the kingdom of heaven. Whosoever therefore shall humble himself as this little child, the same is greatest in the kingdom of heaven. And whoso shall receive one such little child in my name receiveth me.

www.ingramcontent.com/pod-product-compliance
Lightning Source LLC
Chambersburg PA
CBHW040122170426
42811CB00124B/1486